SEO: Search Engine Optimization for beginners – SEO made simple with SEO secrets to rank your website in the top of Google

Table of Contents

Introduction

Thank you for downloading this book entitled *"The Ultimate SEO Guide"*.

This book serves as your all-in-one guide. Through this book, you will find everything you have to know about basic SEO. You will discover proven strategies and steps that will enable you to benefit much from optimizing your website, such as:

- Know how search engines work so you can use your knowledge to do the right things that will increase the visibility of your website to your target market

- Unlock your difficulties such as increasing your understanding of the mathematical formula search engines use in ranking and listing your website

- Master the basic steps in optimizing your content

- Rank for the right keywords

- Use the factors that influence search engine ranking to your advantage

- Stick to ethical strategies in building your links

- Enable your mobile users to enjoy your optimized site

- Track your progress to focus on your best practices and to retool, if necessary

- Clear misconceptions and myths surrounding SEO to prevent roadblocks in achieving your goals

- Profit from the best practices of SEO experts

These and more await you,

So start reading this book right now, so you can apply the strategies. Put the content of this book into profitable use and you'll surely enjoy the rewards.

Are you ready for your ultimate SEO guide?

Chapter 1: Know How Search Engines Work

Search engine optimization (SEO) is the process of modifying certain parts of your website to make it friendly to the search engines and relevant to your traffic (site visitors). The goal of optimizing your website is to make it rank higher, preferably to appear on page one of the search engine results page (SERP).

Purpose of SEO

The purpose of search engine optimization is to increase the visibility of your site to (1) the search engines; and ultimately to your (2) targeted traffic. Let not the words "search engine" mislead you. SEO is not just about tweaking your website for the search engines, but also and more importantly, making it useful and valuable to your traffic.

What Search Engines Are for

Search engines are the tools that searchers use to find websites such as yours that can satisfy their needs or wants. Most online users search for information or content that they can use as solutions to their needs or wants.

Major Players

You will find several search engines on the internet, but the major players are the following: Google, MSN Bing, and Yahoo Search. Among these three, Google remains to be the king of the search engines. In fact, the word "Google" has become synonymous with "search it on the web" such that when a user wants to find something online, he is often told to "Google it".

Main Functions

The main functions of search engines are:

1. Crawling web content for indexing
2. Providing online users solutions or answers to their searches

Search engines perform their functions 24/7 all year round.

How Search Engines Work

How search engines work revolve on their two main functions just mentioned. To index content (web pages, files, documents, videos, and other media), each of the search engines sends their "crawlers" "spiders" or "bots" to do the job.

For instance, Google has its "Googlebot" to crawl the web non-stop for indexing. The crawlers tell the search engines what they can access from your website and index accordingly. Indexing is necessary to determine what will appear on the search engine results. You can control, however, what Googlebot can access from your website.

The path that search engine bots use to crawl and index sites is through links. These links provide the bots easy access to the gazillion of content available on the internet. It is also through links that they will find your web pages, read the code, store information found in your pages for later retrieval as the search need arises.

To store the information, search engines have put up datacenters across the world. These centers are home to countless machines that process all the information crawled and indexed by bots. This is why online users searching for content can immediately see results instantaneously.

Responding to search queries is the other main function of search engines. Up to this moment, most users connect to the World Wide Web to search for information. They do this through the search engines. Users type or encode their queries on the search bar of their preferred search engines, and the latter will put up the results in just a second's fraction. How they show the results depends on two things:

1. Relevance or usefulness to users' queries
2. Ranking according to relevance as search engines see it

Thus, the search engines display the answers to users' queries on their search results page according to rank based on perceived relevance. They then display clickable links that will bring the users to their destination where they can find answers or solutions to their queries.

In the next chapter, you will learn about how search engines determine relevance, which is their primary basis for search ranking. The focus is on Google ranking being the king of the search engines. Nonetheless, you will also find tips on how to improve your rankings in Bing and Yahoo search engine results.

Chapter 2: How Google Algorithm Impacts SEO

From the previous chapter, you have learned that the search engines respond to queries from online users by showing results according to relevance. It used to be that the search engines consider a site relevant if it contains the keywords that searchers use in their queries.

Today, however, there is more to relevance than just using the right words. Search engines have modified their ways of determining relevance to make sure that the sites that appear in their results page are worth searching for by users. They are now focusing on displaying results that are relevant, important, useful, and valuable to searchers, who after all, are the most important consumers of the search results.

What Is Algorithm

Search engines use their respective mathematical formula/equations or set of rules to crawl, index, rank, and display sites in their SERPs. No two engines have the same algorithm, as each formula is unique. Algorithm determines the reasons and the methods search engines arrive at their search results rankings.

Following their algorithms, search engines are able to distinguish sites with genuine and relevant content from spam or junk sites. While the set of rules differ from one search engine to another, they share some common factors.

Common Factors

Here are the things that are common to search engines:

- Relevance – all search engines are looking for and measuring the relevancy of the pages their bots crawl.

  Search engine bots or spiders check whether the sites are: (a) using the right keywords, (b) where these keywords are located, and (c) the frequency of usage of these keywords. The keywords have to be relevant to the search and to the web page content where users can find them.

- Link Building – in ranking websites, all search engines consider off-page factors such as link building. They measure the popularity of web pages through the quantity and quality of backlinks.

Importance of Google Algorithm

Inarguably, Google is the king of search engines and continues to dominate the search engine world today. The primary reason is their exceptional algorithmic formula. Bing has bumped off Yahoo Search to come next to Google in superiority.

Google algorithm is superior because through it, what users see on the search results pages are what they really need or want. Google is able to pull up the most relevant answers to searchers' queries. Users can expect Google to pull up sites whose content users will find most relevant and valuable to the keywords they have entered.

Thus, it is safe to say that all webmasters or site administrators are targeting to rank prominently in Google's SERP. They optimize their websites to earn the best favor from the Google algorithm with the hope of earning a higher SERP ranking. Prominent ranking in Google's SERP means increase in visibility and more website visitors or traffic.

Google Updates

Google continues to update their algorithm to ensure users they get the most relevant and valuable results. If the focus before is on the use of keywords and popularity of the site, Google algorithmic updates have created significant impact on how to do search engine optimization. In the following paragraphs, you'll learn about the major updates

Google Panda

Perhaps, the major update that eventually shook up the way webmasters or site administrators perform search engine optimization happened sometime in February 2011 with the release of Google Panda.

The update encouraged websites to improve the quality of their content and avoid "thin content". This has affected 11.8% of searches or queries with Google cracking down and penalizing sites that are publishing low quality, duplicate, or keyword-stuffed content.

Article directories were the hardest hit. Some of the most popular directories witnessed how their rankings dropped considerably.

This drop has prompted them to modify their own rules to conform to the Panda update so that they can regain their SERP ranks and readership. Their rules favor end users, as their readers or subscribers can enjoy highly relevant content.

Google Penguin

In April of 2012, Google rolled its next major update, the Penguin. While Panda influenced on-page optimization (content), Penguin's impact is on off-page optimization (link building).

With the implementation of the Penguin algorithmic update, Google started to crack down on sites that are employing black hat (unethical) techniques to rank high in the SERP. This includes schemes in link building as well as keyword stuffing.

Google Penguin has affected 3%+ of searches or queries, with pornographic and gaming sites as the biggest SERP ranking losers. This update intends to discourage and stop webmasters and site administrators from carrying out unethical SEO practices, and encourage building and earning of quality and genuine backlinks.

Google Hummingbird

In August of 2013, Google released a new algorithm Hummingbird aimed at recognizing full-question queries. With Google intending to enhance user experience in searching for content online, the release of the Hummingbird makes searching with Google conversational. This new algorithm has affected more or less 90% of searches across the world.

The release is to boost Google's voice technology search, a strategy to capture the mobile population. Hence, keywords are not the only thing that matters to rank high in the SERP, but Google also highlights the importance of human interests in providing users with high quality content. The king of the search engines will also consider the purpose of the users, and not just the keywords they use, to show them relevant results ranked accordingly.

Google Pigeon

The newest algorithm update by Google is the Pigeon, rolled out on 24 July 2014. The update is applicable to web search as well as map search and affects only local searches in English in the US. Pigeon intends to strengthen and improve local queries.

If you are already providing your traffic with high quality content, then you just have to continue with your practice. At the same time, see to it that your content is more specific to the locality where your targeted users are or where your business operates. If you still have not, it is time for you to claim and optimize your My Business listing.

Assessing the Impact

Every time Google releases its algorithm updates, it sends webmasters/site administrators scampering to modify their SEO campaigns and tweak their websites.

Google Tips

- When creating and optimizing your web pages, think about your targeted traffic first before you think about Google or other search engines.

- Your web content should be useful to your visitors. Use keywords prudently and not just to rank high on SERPs.

- Create title tags for your pages using the right keywords. Make sure that the tags describe the content on the pages accurately.

If your pages show on Google's SERP, your title tag will also appear on the first line. Users normally read the first line to decide whether to click on your link or not.

You don't really have to do the same thing. Understand that the goal of Google in releasing its algorithms updates or changes is to encourage websites to put their best feet forward to provide users (website visitors/traffic) the best content possible.

Therefore, if you are consistent in uploading high quality content relevant to your traffic, and you stay away from black hat techniques in optimizing your website, then you're good to go. You should not worry about modifying your website all the time Google releases updates, but it is important that you monitor them to comply as the need arises.

You may want to consider outsourcing your SEO needs, if it means freeing you or your staff to focus on your core activities. Weigh the pros and cons and if the benefits exceed the cost, then by all means, choose the best SEO expert or company whose services you can afford to enlist.

You may want to check the site that lists the top 50 SEO company rankings of 2014 as one of your resources. You will find several other sites of similar function that you can use to guide you in making the best decision should your decide in favor of outsourcing your SEO requirements.

Chapter 3: Optimizing Your Web Pages & Content

From the previous chapter, you have learned about how algorithm influences search engine optimization. In this chapter, you'll get to know more about the proven strategies and procedures in optimizing your web pages and content taking into consideration Google's major algorithmic updates.

The Basics
Unique Page Titles
Page titles matter to search engines. Typically, titles allow the search engines to determine the content of your pages. Search engines will display your title tags in their SERP to give users an idea of what to expect when they go to your site.

See to it that each of your pages has a unique title so that the search engines can easily distinguish one page from another. In line with Google Panda, your title tags should describe accurately what your traffic could read or view from the pages.

Your title tags should not be lengthy, though. Brief yet concise and descriptive titles, between 50-60 characters, are the best since the search engines will only trim lengthy titles to make them fit in the allocated space.

Keep in mind that your website visitors are human beings and not robots, and therefore create your titles for their benefit. For optimization purposes, format your titles for search engine crawlers.

Main keyword │ Secondary keyword │ Brand

Using the right keywords is also important since search engines highlight them as they match users' queries. Your site will earn more traffic because of greater visibility in the search engine results page.

Meta Descriptions
Meta tags are codes that tell the search engines what the content of your page is. They also provide users snippets of your site, which users can see below the title tag (blue link). If your Meta description contains keywords that match users queries, these keywords will show in highlighted texts.

Here is an example of a Meta descriptive tag:

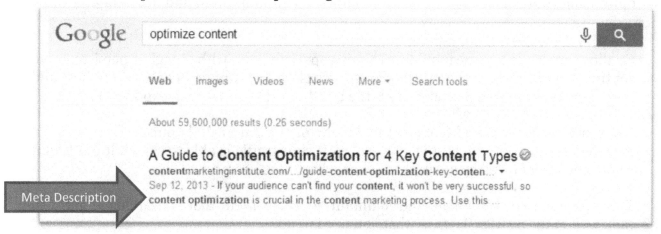

In creating your optimized Meta description, consider these tips:

- Include the right keywords that will catch the attention of your targeted traffic. Make sure these keywords summarize the content of your web pages, though in consideration of the algorithm.

- Create a unique Meta description for each of your pages. Limit your Meta description to 156 characters or less. Your description should also show your traffic your unique message or value proposition.

Easy Site Navigation

Your navigation enables your traffic to get to the page(s) that contains the information or content they need or want from your site. Through your navigation, the search engines get to understand your content according to importance.

Therefore, in designing your navigation, see to it that:

1. Users will be able to switch pages easily and conveniently, e.g. from a page containing general information to a page that has specific or detailed information.

2. Prefer to use text links for navigation. This makes it easier for search engine crawlers to move from one page to another and understand the content of your site. Text links are also favorable to users of mobile browsers.

Two things to keep in mind in designing your navigation: (1) make it easy; and (2) keep it simple.

Optimizing Your Content

You need to make your content searchable to your targeted traffic. Therefore, optimizing your content for the search engines is both important and necessary.

Quality Content

Quality content is non-negotiable. This is especially true with Google's persistency in continuously perking up its SERP through releasing algorithmic updates every now and then. The ultimate goal is to give users the best browsing and search experience.

You must also understand that creating killer content is useless if your traffic is not able to search for it. Your content is also useless if your traffic is able to search it but find it irrelevant and not worthy at all.

Therefore, you need to create and maintain quality content that is searchable and will rank well in the SERPs. Here is what you need to do:

- Upload unique content that is fresh and easy to read.
- Humanize your content. Keep in mind that the most important readers of your content are your traffic and not the search engine crawlers.
- However, make your content easy to index by the crawlers, and this is through using the text format (HTML). Only use non-text format when they are necessary. If you need to upload images or videos, include text descriptions or transcript of the file(s).

Optimizing Images

Images are essential to web pages. Your website will be drab and boring if your visitors only see texts. Some people also learn best visually. However, images can also compromise the speed of your website and may not be friendly to crawlers.

Optimizing is the solution to resolve the problem. Here are the basic things to optimize your images:

- Create brief but concise description for your images (whether you are uploading photos or graphics). Build your description around keywords as much as possible or where appropriate.
- For images that you will use as links, make sure that you include an alt (alternate) text. This will increase the crawlers' understanding of the page(s) where your image(s) would like to link. Again, keep the alt text short and accurate.

Appropriate Use of Heading Tags

Heading tags are one way to organize the content you have uploaded on any of your web pages. These tags come in six sizes, from <h1> to <h6>. However, the most important tag is your <h1>.

In the hierarchy of heading tags, the <h1> tells your traffic what content they can expect to view or read from the page.

Thus, your <h1> is what the search engine crawlers will look at to index and evaluate your page for ranking. If you optimize your <h1> tag, it can boost your ranking in the SERPs. Here's how to find out if you are using your <h1> tag correctly:

- You must have only one (1) <h1> tag on your page. If you have more than one, convert it into sub-headings such as <h2>.

- Your <h1> tag should include your main keyword for the page. It should also match the ones you used for your title tag and Meta description.

- Use headings only when they contribute to the organization of your web pages. They should serve their purpose of making it easier for your traffic to scan your web pages and determine what content they are about to read/view.

Chapter 4: Ranking for the Right Keywords

Ranking high in the search engine results page (SERP) involves largely the use of the right keywords. Using the right keywords will ensure that your high quality content will also enjoy high visibility in the SERP.

High ranking in the SERP will make your content easily searchable by and accessible to your targeted traffic. In this chapter, you will learn about the proven ways to rank high for the right keywords.

How to Determine the Right Keywords

Keyword Research

In identifying the right keywords to use to rank high in the SERPs, you can benefit much from using tools for keyword research. Using these tools will save you time and effort that you will have to spend otherwise.

An example of these tools is Google's Keyword Planner. The Keyword Planner will help you to (a) find keywords relevant to your website, products or services that you offer; and (b) use its statistics such as search volume to guide you in deciding the keywords to use for your SEO campaigns. You will have to create your AdWords account to be able to access and start using the tool.

To assess the value of your keywords, follow these steps:

1. See to it that your keywords match the content of your website. Your traffic should be able to get their solutions from your site when they find you through these keywords.

2. Test the keywords using the major search engines – Google, Bing, and Yahoo Search. This way, you will get to know your competition or the websites that are already ranking high for your keywords.

3. You have the option to buy traffic for testing from Google AdWords. Testing your keywords will allow you to assess the conversion rate, if your site isn't ranking.

Use of Long Tail Keyword

Most times, you will be better off using long tail keywords instead or popular keywords. The former may be less popular than the latter, but they usually score higher in conversion.

The reason is that long tail keywords are more specific and unique. Searchers who use these keywords are typically those who have pre-need and who are already almost ready to buy the solution or make a purchase.

For example, a searcher using "SEO" as the keyword probably wants information about how search engine optimization works. However, a searcher who uses "most reasonable SEO Company in Nevada" is most likely to avail the services given the right content.

Work Involved

You would also have to consider the work involved when choosing the right keyword. Assess the level of difficulty in making your website rank with the keywords you prefer.

For instance, testing the keyword on Google will show you which websites are already occupying page one of the SERP. If you see that those websites belong to big brands, then it may be a long road for you to get to your destination.

There are tools online that will help you measure the difficulty level of keywords, so that you can make better choices and the best decision.

Using the Right Keywords

When you have already determined the right keywords, the next thing to do is to build your content with these keywords. Again, build your content for your traffic, and use your keywords to rank in the SERPs.

This means, your keywords should be your tool to create content that is relevant and valuable to your traffic. You don't stuff your content with the keyword even if they no longer make sense just so you can catch Google's attention.

Do you remember the Panda? Keyword stuffing will only earn Google's ire and may send it penalizing your website. You don't want this to happen, or you do? On the other hand, creating usable and helpful content will earn for you Google's respect and it will reward you accordingly such as promoting your rank.

Unique Keywords for Each Page

Make it a point to assign unique keywords for each of your web pages. This will help you (a) avoid duplicating your content; and (b) prevent your traffic from clicking away from your site after viewing a single web page.

Build your internal links. Each of your web pages should discuss its own topic, use different keywords to create your content for each page. Interconnect the pages through appropriate links.

Chapter 5: Key Factors that Influence Your SERP Ranking

Search engines continuously find ways to produce better search results. One clear example is Google with its algorithmic updates. In optimizing your web pages, it is to your advantage to familiarize yourself with the key factors that influence your ranking given the constant efforts of search engines to improve their SERPs.

Content Quality

Content is perhaps the biggest influencer, as this is the main reason the online population would use the search engines. Internet users are looking for legitimate, reliable, and high quality content. If you are meeting and satisfying this need, then the search engines will reward you with high ranking.

How Search Engines Know if Your Content Is High Quality

Search engines may have different algorithms, but there are standards when it comes to determining the quality of content.

- User Engagement – search engines monitor how users interact with their search results page. For instance, which among the links will you click first from the search results? Studies reveal that the first 5-10 links usually gets the most clicks.

  Search engines will then determine your engagement with the links you see in the search results page. For instance, if you have clicked on the first link and then within just a few seconds, you go back to check the next link, then the search engines will interpret this as dissatisfaction on your part.

- Links – search engines love links as they indicate how popular and authoritative sites are. Typically, you will only link with a site if the content is useful and relevant to your own content. Hence, links indicate the quality of content that websites maintain.

- Algorithm – the mathematical equations and formula can mimic how human beings would identify sites as low in quality. Google's algorithm, for instance, can now predict accurately how to evaluate sites with low quality content. This technology is why Google has released the Panda and its series of updates.

Keyword Usage

Keyword usage remains to be an influencing factor to rank high in the search engines. As discussed previously, though, keywords should make sense and integrated into your content primarily written for human beings.

The search engines also consider "relevant keywords" and "proof keywords" in ranking websites for their SERPs. Both types of keywords help the search engines distinguish legitimate content from spam.

Freshness of Content

Search engines highly favor fresh content. This is why you will find blogs as among the higher-ranking sites owing to their nature of updating their sites constantly. Fresh content is non-negotiable for the following queries: (a) news, (b) current events, and (c) recurring events.

Google does not only measure freshness in terms of how old your website is, but it also considers the changes you have made overtime. If you are consistent in uploading new content or updating your existing content, then you'll earn a higher score that can push your site higher in the ranking.

Website Usability

The factors that make a good website will also enable the website to enjoy high ranking in the SERPs. You just have to guard against over optimizing your site. Ensuring that your site is highly useful to your targeted traffic is enough to earn for you the search engines' good favor.

You should be able to give your traffic a different browsing experience with the critical goal of increasing conversion rate. As soon as your traffic clicks your link from the search results, make their experience worthwhile. You should avoid wasting their time and attention; and you should prevent them from leaving your site right away and look for their solution elsewhere.

Two things to achieve this: (1) provide them with high quality content they need or want; and (2) make your site user-friendly. If you can turn your site into a "one-stop-shop" of sorts, then the more likely it is for you to delight your traffic and the search engines resulting with increase in traffic and conversion as well as moving up in the search engine results page.

Usability Factors

In making your website usable for both your targeted traffic and the search engines, consider these:

- Your website must be able to meet the expectations of the searchers. When your targeted traffic arrives at your site, they should be able to find what they are searching for and complete any necessary tasks easily.

- Increase the efficiency of your traffic in doing their business on your site. Whatever it is that they need to do or to complete- your site should be able to allow them to do it the least time possible.

- Learning curve should be low such that your traffic should be able to use your website intuitively. Your traffic should not spend much time in learning how to use the functionalities of your site.

User Satisfaction

Satisfaction of your traffic comes when your website is able to deliver them what they need or want without difficulty. If you make it rewarding and satisfying for your traffic to visit your site, you can expect them to come back often, bookmark your web pages, recommend your site to their social connections, share your content, and more.

To improve user experience and increase satisfaction, consider doing the following:

- Create a structure that will make it easy and convenient for you traffic to understand, navigate, and use your website.

- See to it that your keywords have corresponding high quality content that your traffic will appreciate and value.

- Build your website around relevant content for your traffic first. Use a search engine-friendly format to increase visibility of your site to your targeted traffic.

Keep in mind that if your website content is irrelevant to your traffic, your visitors will leave. Without traffic, you cannot expect the search engines to rank your site to your advantage. It is just this simple.

Chapter 6: Ethical Strategies to Build Links

From the earlier times of the internet to the present, search engines have been using links to determine the popularity, authority, and credibility of websites. The more links your website earns, the better its chances to climb the SERP ranks.

Link building is one of the major factors that can sway ranking in your favor or against your favor. In fact, the search engine factors for ranking are mostly link building-based. From patterns, search engines observe that sites maintaining high quality content earn quality links while junk sites or spam will rarely earn quality links.

How Google Updates Changed the Way to Do Link Building

Back to the earlier times of SEO, it was easy to build links. Several websites, in fact, resort to black hat techniques such as building spam links, and enjoy watching their sites soar swiftly in the SERPs.

While black hat techniques still exist, Google has successfully stripped them of their power that these techniques have practically become toothless. Unless you want to see your website penalized and your ranking steeply dropped, then you must avoid using black hat techniques.

April 24, 2012 saw the release of Google Penguin, an anti-spam update of the search engine's core algorithm. It was an update intended to crack down spammers and all those sites violating the search engine's guidelines.

With the release of Penguin, several sites plummeted and lost their traffic, especially gaming and pornographic sites where you will find the most number of spam links.

Therefore, you should always think about this when building links to optimize your site: search engines favor quality over quantity. Earning authentic quality links will only happen when you implement ethical strategies.

Build Links that Rank High In the Search Engines

While search engines perceive links per se as favorable, search engines still have a different valuation of these links based on the these principles, according to Rand Fishkin in his blog article for MOZ:

- Links may be considered as votes
- Initially, search engines consider all votes (links) as equal

- In implementing the algorithm, web pages receiving more votes climb the hierarchy of importance
- Eventually, the value and power of any web page's vote will have to depend on where it is on the hierarchy. To illustrate: Vote = function of importance/#of votes casted

What you can do to earn valuable links:

- Place your links strategically in your HTLM Code (this is the hidden code behind your texts and other content). The higher your links are in the code, the more valuable they become to the search engines.

- Focus your attention on building external links rather than links within your web pages. External links reflect how trustworthy your content is to other websites.

- Earn links from trusted sites. Examples are links from seed sites (sites that have earned a manual mark from search engines as trustworthy), or sites liked from seed sites, related websites, and social networking sites.

- Create links within the content instead of outside of the content (e.g. sidebars, footers). Links within the content are more natural.

- Build links with domains that are more popular.

Avoid at all cost spam links, as they will only pull down your ranking regardless of your other trusted links.

Basic Steps in Launching Your Campaign
To launch your link building campaign, follow these steps:

1. Review your website to make sure that its content is useful, relevant, and worthy of linking. You have two options in creating your content: (a) you can create it yourself or your staff; or (b) you can outsource your content requirements to an SEO Company. Whichever option you choose, see to it that the result is the production of high quality content for your website.

2. Find information about potential websites that can become part of your link-building network. You want to link with and earn links from trusted websites. To do that, you have to explore sites that are:

   a) Related to your website – these sites typically have content that caters to or satisfies the needs and wants of your targeted traffic

   b) Ranked as trustworthy by the search engines

c) Influencers or credible and highly authoritative

d) Constantly linking with the competition

3. Create a structure for the information you have gathered. For instance, you can use a spreadsheet and categorize your potential link partners into: (a) natural links (dependent on the quality of your content); (b) manual linking (convincing other sites they will benefit from linking with your site). You will also be able to monitor your campaign easily with a spreadsheet as one of your tools.

4. Start reaching out to your potential partners. To do this:

   a) Leverage on the social media to connect with site owners or administrators. Social media allows you to build relationship, which is a strong foundation for your partnership.

   b) Keep track of your outreach. Know your progress towards your final goals of building quality link with your partner(s) and nurturing your relationship with the owner(s) or administrator(s).

   c) Delegate if you have a team that works on link building. Distribute and assign tasks to the right persons in your team. This will increase the efficiency of achieving your goals in link building.

5. Follow through. Maintain your communication with site owners/administrators and continue building your relationship. Allot about 30 minutes to an hour a day for this purpose. You can use reliable software, but see to it that you also humanize your interaction with your link-building network.

Proven Ways to Build Links
Convert Your Customers into Links
You can earn quality links from your satisfied or repeat customers. For instance, as part of your rewards program, you can give out graphic badges that your customers can display on their own websites, social media accounts, or blogs. These badges, usually a representation of pride and accomplishment, should link back to your website.

Create Viral Content
It is difficult to resist sharing viral content. A content that is contagious and spreads rapidly is one of the most effective ways to earn links. Here is how you can come up with viral content:

- Find out what interests your target traffic the most. Use this as a topic for your viral content.

- Focus on creating positive content instead of negative content. While the latter can easily catch attention, results are short-lived. Positive content makes for long-lasting impression.

- Make your content useful. At the same time, the content should appeal to the emotions. Studies show that consumers are generally emotional buyers. Hence, appealing to their emotions is an effective method to get them to respond to your call(s) to action.

- Be sure to tell your audience how to use your content and what they can benefit from using it. This will lower or eliminate the resistance, and increase the chances of them using your content, benefiting from its use, and feeling gratified that will trigger them to share and recommend your content.

- Consider stimulating these emotions when creating your content:

    o Positive emotions – awe, joy, surprise
    o Negative emotions – anger, anxiety
    o Neutral – fear, lust

These emotions never fail to trigger response from people. Adding these emotions to your content will surely make your audience react, talk about it, and share it to their connections.

Blog Your Content

Build links through blogging. Search engines favor blogging owing to the freshness of content. Matt Cutts, a Google expert engineer, in an interview with the USA Today, recommends blogging as one of the best methods to build links and earn higher ranking in Google's SERP. Blogging enables you to earn backlinks as well as to offer links.

Build links naturally and avoid buying or paying for your links. This will enable you to enjoy long-term benefits, instead of short-lived results. More importantly, building your links naturally will save you from the risks of earning the ire of Google and the other search engines that will make them impose the applicable sanction or penalty.

Chapter 7: Optimizing Your Mobile Site

Considering the continued growth of the mobile population, most site owners/administrators are also going mobile. If you're like them, chances are you already have your mobile site up and running or you have implemented the responsive design for your website.

In this chapter, you'll learn about how to optimize your mobile site to rank higher in the search engines. As the mobile trend continues to get bigger, you'll also be able to do proper optimization of your site with the basic information you'll find here.

Check If Google Has Indexed Your Site

One of the first things you need to do is to <u>check if Google and other search engines have already indexed your mobile site</u>. If it returns unfavorable result, you may want to check the following:

- If your site is new, submit a mobile sitemap to Google to alert it of your site's existence. Otherwise, you should check if the search engines are able to crawl your site for indexing.

- Check your site's accessibility. Allow search engines to access your site so that their bots/spiders/crawlers can do their job.

- Ensure that your URL (site address) is recognizable by the search engines. Each of your web pages has its own URL and therefore you need to check the URLs or all of your web pages.

Focus on the Basics

In designing your site, put premium on reliability and accuracy of the site over sophistication. Focus on the basics, such as the following:

- Create relevant content that search engines can crawl and index.
- Images, videos, and other media as well as your links should all be working properly.
- See to it that your redirects lead users to the right page. Avoid setting your redirects to your home page.
- All your content must be available to users and prevent your site to display error messages or mobile 404 (content is unavailable).
- Get rid of click-to-leave ads, if any, on your site. This is regardless of the presence on your desktop.

Responsive Design

You have the option to shift to a responsive design that will save you from creating different versions of your website. The design uses same code for your website, but it shifts its format when users access your site from their mobile devices. Hence, it saves your website from showing errors or distortions, and at the same time preserves user satisfaction in browsing your site.

The bottom line here is that your website must be simple enough to convert into mobile site as necessary. If you need to run your website with multiple functions and complex menus, then shifting to a responsive design may not be practical or suitable for you.

Understand Your Audience

There is a difference in browsing behavior between a mobile audience and a web audience. This is mainly because mobile browsers are using their devices with features different from conventional computers.

For instance, the display screen is definitely smaller than typical computer display screens. Another difference is the keypad-, which is smaller than laptop keyboards or desktop keyboards.

Because of their smaller screens, mobile users prefer smaller chunks of texts. If they have to resize the display or adjust the zoom, users are most likely to leave your site and look for another site.

Typical to mobile users is the use of touchscreen as well as voice search, which changes the way users search for content on their mobile devices. When searching using voice technology, users often do it by asking questions. This has prompted Google to release the Hummingbird, as discussed in Chapter 2 of this book.

Why Time Matters More

Time becomes non-negotiable for mobile users. This is because users usually do their searches while on the go, in between conversations, or while they can squeeze just enough time to do their searches. Therefore, mobile users want their answers quick.

In view of the extraordinary importance of time, you are better off tweaking the speed and performance of your site. If you can have your site load within just a second or less, the better it is for you to earn and maintain your traffic. It will also do you well to provide content that will quickly answer common queries of your targeted traffic.

Allow your mobile users to get the best browsing experience with your site, and for sure, Google and the rest of the search engines will love you for it. If you wish to explore all the details about this, you will benefit much from Google Mobile Playbook.

Chapter 8: Monitoring & Measuring Your Progress

Keeping track of your progress in optimizing your website for the search engines is necessary so that you can identify your best practices and improve areas that need improvement. Monitoring and measuring your SEO campaigns keep you closer to your ultimate goal of success.

While you can set up your own metrics for measuring your progress, you will find from this chapter the top standard metrics that site administrators/webmasters use to determine progress. Through these metrics, you'll find out if your SEO campaigns are effective or not.

Your Ranking in the SERP

Obviously, checking your current ranking in the search results page (SERP) will show you the progress of your campaigns. Your ranking indicates how well you are implementing your SEO strategy.

It is also a good practice to monitor keyword ranking, so you can find out if the keywords you are using for your SEO campaigns are still the best keywords to rank higher in the SERPs.

Invest on keywords that rank on page one of Google and other major search engines such as Bing and Yahoo Search. Use Chapter 4 of this book as a guide on how to decide and use the right keywords to improve your ranking on the SERPs.

Targeted Traffic

Measuring and monitoring your progress does not begin and end with your SERP ranking. Not because you rank on page one of Google means that, your SEO campaign is successful. You have to consider your traffic. Are you getting the right kind of traffic for your website?

Thus, you need to monitor and measure the volume and quality of your site visitors. You can do this more accurately, effectively, and efficiently with the use of tools such as Google Analytics.

Volume of Your Traffic

If you are progressing with your search engine optimization campaigns, then you should be able to witness the constant surge of your traffic volume. This is especially true if you are able to rank on page one of Google's SERP. Studies show that 90% + of the traffic goes to the sites listed on page one of Google search results.

Quality of Your Traffic

The kind of traffic that you get from optimizing your website is perhaps more important than volume for lead generation and conversion. Measuring your traffic quality requires your more careful interpretation and analysis of data.

One of the first things that you would like to look at in measuring quality is how user engagement increases conversion. When your traffic spends more time in your website, navigating pages, does this translate to conversion? If your SEO campaign is effective, any increase in your user engagement should also reflect an increase in your lead conversion rate or transactions from your traffic.

If there is an increase in your user engagement, e.g. visitors spending more time in your site, but there is no parallel increase in conversion or your conversion rare slips, then you might want to check your website for any "distraction".

In analyzing statistics, you also need to understand how your keywords relate to the traffic earned from your SEO campaign. For example, if you are an SEO specialist and you are targeting an audience that will enlist your services, it makes sense to use the keywords "optimizing website" or "search engine optimization", especially when these keywords rank high.

The trouble with these keywords however is that:

a) Searchers using these keywords may not necessarily have an interest in hiring an SEO specialist, but are just looking for ways that can help them do SEO themselves;

b) Granting that they may be interested in enlisting the services of an SEO, these searchers are in the exploratory stage and are open to other possibilities or solutions.

In contrast, if you aim for the keywords "affordable SEO services" best SEO Company" or "SEO specialist in Los Angeles", you have a better assurance that the searchers are looking for an SEO specialist that can meet their needs or requirements.

Conversion Rate

You optimize your website for the search engines to not only increase your rank, reach the right kind of traffic, but also and perhaps more importantly to increase your conversion rate.

Be standard definition, conversion happens when your traffic responds favorably to your call(s) to action. You therefore measure your conversation rate by the volume of your traffic that performs your desired action.

You define the action you want your traffic to perform. Therefore, conversion can mean subscribing to your newsletter, downloading your whitepaper, creating an account, enlisting your services, or buying your product. You tie your conversion with your goal(s), and you measure your conversion rate through the action of your traffic on what you need or want them to do.

In monitoring your conversion rate, you will be able to determine the effectiveness of your SEO campaigns. You will know which among your keywords are generating the highest conversion rate and why. You will also know which among your keywords are not converting and why so that you can make the necessary adjustments.

Traffic Behavior

How your traffic behaves is another way to monitor and measure your SEO progress. This includes the following:

- The time traffic spends in your website - are your visitors spending considerable time in your website, or do they leave your website soon as they arrive.

- The number of web pages your visitors view – are they looking at your home page or landing page only or do they also browse your other pages?

- What they do with your content – are your visitors sharing your content to their social networks? Do they interact with you through commenting or bookmarking your content?

From the behavior of your website visitors, you will know what works and what doesn't with your SEO strategy. You can then focus on implementing your best practices, and retool or discard those that do not work.

Chapter 9: Let Go of Your Misconceptions

Search engine optimization of SEO is no exception when it comes to myths and misconceptions. You need to let go of these, however, as they will only interfere with your good decisions. Through this chapter, you will be able to debunk prevailing myths and clear your misconceptions about optimizing your site for the search engines.

Submitting to Search Engine Directories

Submitting your site along with the keywords you wish to rank for is so ancient practice and now outdated. It is no longer necessary to submit your site, unless the search engines are not able to crawl or recognize you despite your SEO efforts, as discussed in Chapter 7 to check if the search engines are able to index your site.

This ancient practice will not earn for you links that you wish to earn to rank higher in the SERP. You are better off building your links naturally and earning your links through providing internet users with high quality, relevant, and trustworthy content.

Links Are Superior than Content

If you believe than building links is far better than building your content to rank high in the search engines, then you just have to change your belief. Link building and content go hand-in-hand when doing SEO.

What is true is that earning quality links can give you better ranking than earning more links with disregard for quality. The ideal is to find the balance of quantity and quality. You can earn more quality links with quality content.

If you consistently provide your traffic with quality content, you will be able to build quality links naturally. This will make your site rank higher in the SERPs.

No Need for SEO with Good Content

Is your website home to high quality content? Then, you don't need search engine optimization (SEO). This sounds legit. However, while good content can make your visitors stay in your website, SEO is what is going to bring them there in the first place.

You will have to make your good content discoverable by the right audience. You want to reach the people who are most likely to respond favorably to your call to action. This you can do through optimizing your web pages for the search engines.

Therefore, you need to include keywords that rank in your good content. These keywords are what your potential customers are using when they use Google or the other search engines for their queries. Your content should be able to answer their queries, and your SEO should be able to lead your customers to your site.

Meta Keywords Tag

Meta keywords tag is necessary to rank in the SERPs. This is true when you are talking about ancient SEO or the pre-Panda days. With the release of Google's Panda, however, this has changed and using Meta keywords became obsolete.

For one thing, Meta keywords tag is a good element for abuse. Spammers love using it to stuff their sites with keywords. It was an effective way to rank, until Google and the rest of the search engines discovered the scheme.

If you are to use any Meta tag, make that the Meta description and title tags. Check the basics on chapter 3 of this book for tips on how to benefit from the use of these tags.

Keyword Density Matters

There is a prevailing belief that keyword density is important to rank high in the search engines. The reason is that a number of SEO tools still use the concept of density as metric. However, if you understand Google algorithmic updates clearly, you would know that keyword density should not matter.

What matters is the relevancy and usability of your content. If you are writing good content with an intelligent use of your keywords, then you're good to go.

Spend for Paid Search

Why spend for something without proof that it actually delivers results of making your site rank in the SERPs? You would not need paid search advertising as long as you are doing your SEO correctly: producing searchable quality content that benefits your target audience, users, or potential customers.

You don't have to buy keywords that rank and then stuff it to your content. No one loves spam except the spammers. One of the biggest reasons Google is the king of search engines is because of it is able to get rid of spam more effectively than other search engines do. With Google's algorithm updates, it has become tedious and difficult to manipulate search engine rankings.

SEO is About Ranking High on SERP

Ranking high on SERP is not the only metric to determine your SEO success. Optimizing your website is a combination of several things, and determining your success depends on several metrics, as you have learned from the previous chapter.

Page rank as a metric lets the search engines measure how relevant and useful your site is to searchers. Certainly, it's an important metric, but it does not single-handedly define SEO. Other metrics are of equal importance such as conversion rate, user behavior and engagement, and traffic generation.

Chapter 10: Best SEO Practices

In this chapter, you will find the best practices in search engine optimization that have delivered proven high performance results. Use these practices as your guide to increase your chances of success in achieving your goals.

On-Page Optimization

This involves creating site content and structure relevant to users and friendly to the search engines. Here are the best practices in optimizing your content and structure:

Unique Content

Ensure that the content in your web pages is unique and relevant to your traffic. Your content should be able to give your traffic the answers to their questions that have prompted them to use Google or other search engines.

You should structure your web pages in such a way that:

- Each of your pages should have a short but descriptive title.
- They should also have their own Meta description tags allowing the search engines and searchers to know what the page is about in summary.
- Your web pages should have their own URL or address that is easy to remember by users and recognizable by the search engines.
- Your site navigation must be simple and easy to use.

Your content should address primarily the needs and wants of your users or traffic. Use a search-engine friendly format and structure to make your content searchable.

Optimize Images

Images that you upload on your site must serve their purposes. To optimize your images, here are the best practices:

- Each of your images should have its own unique file name and alternative text (alt attribute).
- The file name and alt attribute for your images should be short yet concise.
- When using any of your images as a link, be sure to accompany it with an alt text that will enable search engine crawlers to recognize it.
- Provide a sitemap for your images.

Avoid Spam

Search engines hate spam as much as users do. This is why Google continues to be the leader of the search engines because it fights spam with persistence.

Don't Stuff Keywords

Keyword stuffing is a favorite technique of spammers to manipulate search engine rankings. However, the search engines have set their algorithms to detect and fight keyword stuffing, and the results have been successful.

Instead of stuffing keywords, use them intelligently to create meaningful content that your users will appreciate and value. You have to go back to the principle of creating content for human beings and not for search engines.

Do Not Cloak Your Content

The content that you present to the search engines should the same content that you show your traffic. There should be no hidden content especially when hiding it for ranking in the SERPs.

In certain instances, search engines may allow cloaking, but only for valid purposes. To know when cloaking is valid, read Rand Fishkin's article on the Moz Blog. Unless it's truly necessary, you are better off to avoid cloaking.

Check Your Site for Spam

Make it a habit to monitor and check your site for spam. Here are some of the signals that your website may contain spam:

- The search engines are not able to crawl and index your page because of errors.
- Your ranking drops when search engines update or change their algorithms.
- Any change in your site's content carry the risk of spamming and this also changes how search engines perceive your website.

Off-Page Optimization

In SEO, off-page optimization involves off-site factors that influence your listing in the SERPs. Link building is an example of off-page optimization. Here are the best practices.

Find the Good Balance of Quantity and Quality

Getting more links with disregard for quality will not earn for you higher ranking in the SERPs. Instead, it can only expose your site to penalties as the search engines detect the use of black hat techniques or unethical practices.

Instead of focusing on earning more links, pay attention to the quality of links. The ideal thing is to balance quantity and quality.

Never Manipulate the Process

To protect your site against manipulative linking, as a rule, avoid the following:

- Joining programs for reciprocal link exchange - These programs usually have a common purpose of inflating link popularity. Unfortunate for these programs, the search engines are implementing highly effective ways to detect manipulations and are so far succeeding in their campaigns against this practice.

- Using link schemes such as "farming" and "networking" – This involves creating websites or blogs with low quality content or junk content for the purpose of artificial inflation of popularity. Google has released its Penguin algorithm to take care of cracking down these schemes.

- Paying for your links – will only make you spend your hard-earned money with no guarantee that you will get your desired results. Invest in improving the quality of your content to earn links naturally.

Leverage on Social Media
Best practices include:

- Getting to know the rules and protocols of social media sites and choosing which sites are best to serve your purposes
- Respect the privacy of your social connections. Make sure the links you provide your connections will benefit them.

Use social media to promote your site. This way, you can increase the awareness and understanding of more people to your site and the hard work to provide them with the best content possible. Help your targeted traffic to discover your site by leveraging on the social media.

Grow Your External Links
It pays to pay attention more to growing your external links than your internal links. To increase the value of your links, here are the best practices:

- Provide high quality content that would make other sites want to link to your content.
- Earn links from seed sites or trusted sites.
- Get to know the needs of potential link partner(s), and satisfy those needs to increase the relevancy of your content to the content of your potential link partner(s).
- Create well-defined anchor texts for your links.

External links allow the search engines to measure your site's popularity, credibility, relevancy, and authority more reliably. Together with other metrics, if search engine validates the importance of your site to the search population, then they will reward you with greater visibility in their search results listing.

Conclusion

It is a good decision to invest in search engine optimization, especially if you want to strengthen the importance of your brand. People still use the internet primarily to get information. Their main tool to send queries and get answers is to use the search engines. Hence, optimizing your website for the search engines is crucial.

Through an optimized website, you will be able to:

- Increase the visibility of your brand in the search engine results listing
- Reach your targeted traffic through the keywords they use to send their queries online and look for solutions
- Help your targeted traffic find the best solution to their queries from your brand
- Differentiate your brand from your competition and gain your competitive advantage
- Connect with other site administrators or owners related to your business and work together to fulfill the needs and wants of your traffic
- Generate targeted leads and increase their conversion
- Grow your business or brand profitably

Using the content of this book as your ultimate guide in doing SEO will bring you much benefit including but not limited to the following:

- Enhance your ability to make the best choices and the right decisions in SEO
- Use SEO as a cost-effective strategy for higher ROI
- Enable your website to satisfy the needs of the mobile user population
- Let your business move forward and enjoy greater profitability

After digesting the content of this book, the next thing to do is to start implementing the methods, strategies, and steps recommended herewith. See how in using this book as your guide, you will be able to get the results you desire.

Again, I would like to thank you for downloading *"The Ultimate SEO Guide."*